Teen Self-Esteem Workbook

Facilitator Reproducible Self-Assessments, Exercises & Educational Handouts

John J. Liptak, EdD
Ester A. Leutenberg

Illustrated by
Amy L. Brodsky, LISW-S

wholeperson
Stress & Wellness Publishers
Duluth, Minnesota

Whole Person
210 West Michigan Street
Duluth, MN 55802-1908

800-247-6789

books@wholeperson.com
www.wholeperson.com

Teen Self-Esteem Workbook
Facilitator Reproducible Self-Assessments,
Exercises & Educational Handouts

Printed in the United States of America

10 9 8 7 6 5 4 3 2 1

Editorial Director: Carlene Sippola
Art Director: Joy Morgan Dey

Library of Congress Control Number:2011927797
ISBN: 978-1-57025-254-9

Using This Book *(For the professional)*

To be able to reach personal and professional goals, self-esteem is critical. For teens, healthy self-esteem is even more critical, both emotionally and physically. Self-esteem dictates how teens treat and feel about themselves and others, assert themselves, view and act in the world, and take care of their basic needs. Research suggests that low self-esteem can be tied to many mental and physical health issues:

- Aches and pains
- Alcohol abuse
- Angry outbursts
- Anxiety
- Bullying issues (victim, bully, bystander)
- Depression
- Drug use

- Eating disorders
- Fatigue
- Loneliness
- Poor school/work performance
- Relationships
- Stress
- Unhealthy eating

The *Teen Self-Esteem Workbook* is designed to help teens engage in self-reflection, examine their thoughts and feelings that either enhance or detract from healthy self-esteem, and learn effective tools and techniques for building positive feelings of self-esteem and self-worth. This book combines three powerful psychological tools for the management of aggressive thoughts, feelings and behaviors: self-assessment, journaling and role-playing. All to enhance empathy and allow teens to practice self-esteem building strategies.

The *Teen Self-Esteem Workbook* contains five separate sections that will guide the participants toward learning more about themselves and how their self-esteem impacts them.

Teen Self-Esteem Scale helps teens explore their perceptions of themselves and feelings about themselves.

Teen Self-Worth Scale helps teens explore the extent to which they view themselves as valuable and worthy human beings.

Teen Self-Understanding Scale helps teens explore how aware they are of their personal characteristics and attitudes.

Teen Self-Responsibility Scale helps teens explore how much responsibility they assume for what happens in their lives.

Teen Assertiveness Scale helps teens explore how assertive they are in their asking for what they want and need.

Bonus: Enrichment Activities in this section.

(Continued on the next page)

Using This Book *(For the professional, continued)*

Additional Factors

The *Teen Self-Esteem Workbook* deals with many different aspects of self-esteem, including self-worth, self-responsibility, self-awareness, and assertive behavior. Self-esteem is a person's overall evaluation of self-worth and encompasses a person's emotions, thoughts and ways of behaving. For people to make effective decisions and efficiently solve problems, they must have healthy self-esteem. Teens with healthy self-esteem are likely not to simply "follow the crowd," but rather to trust themselves to make decisions that are in their best interest.

Prior to beginning each section, you may want to use the educational handouts toward the end of the section, as an introduction or review for yourself and/or the students.

Use Codes for Confidentiality

Confidentiality is a term for any action that preserves the privacy of people. Because teens completing the activities in this workbook might be asked to answer assessment items and to journal about and explore their relationships, you will need to discuss confidentiality before you begin using the materials in this workbook. Maintaining confidentiality is important as it shows respect for others and allows participants to explore their feelings without hurting anyone's feelings or fearing gossip, harm or retribution.

In order to maintain confidentiality, explain to the participants that they need to assign a code name for each person they write about as they complete the various activities in the workbook. For example, a friend named Joey who enjoys going to hockey games might be titled JLHG (Joey Loves Hockey Games) for a particular exercise. In order to protect their friends' identities, they should not use people's actual names or initials – just codes.

Layout of the Book

The *Teen Self-Esteem Workbook* is designed to be used either independently or as part of an integrated curriculum. You may administer one of the assessments and the journaling exercises to an individual or a group with whom you are working, or you may administer a number of the assessments over one or more days.

Reproducible Pages in the First Five Sections:

❏ **Assessment Instruments** – Self-assessment inventories with scoring directions and interpretation materials offer group facilitators to choose one or more of the activities relevant to their participants.

❏ **Activity Handouts** – Practical questions and activities that prompt self-reflection and promote self-understanding, foster introspection and promote pro-social behaviors.

❏ **Quotations** – Quotations in each section provide insight and promote reflection. Participants will be asked to select one or more of the quotations and journal about what the quotations mean to them.

❏ **Reflective Questions for Journaling** – Self-exploration activities and journaling exercises specific to each assessment will enhance self-discovery, learning, and healing.

❏ **Educational Handouts** – Handouts designed to enhance instruction can be used individually or in groups to promote an understanding of the participants self-esteem, and tools and techniques for enhancing self-esteem.

These pages can be distributed, scanned and converted into masters for overheads or transparencies, projected or written on boards and/or discussed.

Who Should Use This Program?

This book has been designed as a practical tool for helping professionals, such as therapists, counselors, psychologists, teachers, group leaders, etc. Depending on the role of the professional using the *Teen Self-Esteem Workbook* and the specific group's needs, these sections can be used individually or combined for a more comprehensive approach.

Why Use Self-Assessments?

- Self-assessments are important in helping teens develop a healthy self-esteem. Participants engage in these ways to explore personal elements of self-esteem:
- Become aware of the primary motivators that guide their behavior
- Explore and learn to "let go" of troublesome habits and behavioral patterns learned in childhood
- Explore the effects of unconscious childhood messages
- Gain insight and "a wake-up call" for behavioral change
- Focus thinking on behavioral goals for change
- Uncover resources they possess that can help them to cope better with problems and difficult choices
- Explore personal characteristics without judgment
- Develop awareness of personal strengths and weaknesses

Because the assessments are presented in a straightforward and easy-to-use format, individuals can self-administer, score and interpret each assessment at their own pace.

About the Assessments, Journaling Activities and Educational Handouts

Materials in the Assessments, Journaling Activities, and Educational Handouts sections in this book are reproducible and can be photocopied for participants' use. Assessments contained in this book focus on self-reported data and thus are similar to ones used by psychologists, counselors, therapists and career consultants. The accuracy and usefulness of the information provided is dependent on the truthful information that each participant provides. By being honest, participants help themselves to learn about unproductive and ineffective patterns in their lives, and to uncover information that might be keeping them from being as happy or as successful as they might be.

An assessment instrument can provide participants with valuable information about themselves; however, these assessments cannot measure or identify everything. The assessments' purpose is not to pigeonhole certain characteristics, but rather to allow participants to explore all of their characteristics. This book contains self-assessments, not tests. Tests measure knowledge or whether something is right or wrong. For the assessments in this book, there are no right or wrong answers. These assessments ask for personal opinions or attitudes about a topic of importance in the participant's life.

When administering the assessments in this workbook, remember that even though the items are generically written so that they will be applicable to a wide variety of people, all items will not account for every possible variable for every person. No assessments are specifically tailored to one person, so use the assessments to help participants identify negative themes in their lives and to find ways to break the hold of these patterns and their effects.

Advise teen participants taking the assessments that they should not spend too much time trying to analyze the content of the questions; they should think about the questions in general and then spontaneously report how they feel about each one. Whatever the results of the assessment, encourage participants to talk about their findings and their feelings pertaining to what they have discovered about themselves. Talking about issues such as body image and self-worth can be therapeutic and beneficial.

The *Teen Self-Esteem Workbook* sections serve as an avenue for individual self-reflection, as well as group experiences revolving around identified topics of importance. Each assessment includes directions for easy administration, scoring and interpretation. In addition, each section includes exploratory activities, reflective journaling activities, insightful quotations and educational handouts to help participants to discover the extent of their self-esteem, explore their habitual, ineffective ways of viewing themselves, and to define new ways to build a healthy sense of self.

(Continued on the next page)

About the Assessments, Journaling Activities and Educational Handouts *(Continued)*

The art of self-reflection goes back many centuries and is rooted in many of the world's greatest spiritual and philosophical traditions. Socrates, the ancient Greek philosopher, was known to walk the streets engaging the people he met in philosophical reflection and dialogue. He felt that this type of activity was so important in life that he proclaimed, "The unexamined life is not worth living!" The unexamined life is one in which the same routine is continually repeated without ever thinking about its meaning to one's life and how this life really could be lived. However, a structured reflection and examination of beliefs, assumptions, characteristics and patterns can provide a better understanding which can lead to a more satisfying life and career. A greater level of self-understanding about important life skills is often necessary to make positive, self-directed changes in the negative patterns that keep repeating throughout life. The assessments and exercises in this book can help promote this self-understanding. Through involvement with the in-depth activities, each participant claims ownership in the development of positive patterns.

Journaling is an extremely powerful tool for enhancing self-discovery, learning, transcending traditional problems, breaking ineffective life and career habits, and helping people to heal from psychological traumas of the past. From a physical point of view, writing reduces stress and lowers muscle tension, blood pressure and heart rate levels. Psychologically, writing reduces feelings of sadness, depression and general anxiety, and it leads to a greater level of life satisfaction and optimism. Behaviorally, writing leads to enhanced social skills, emotional intelligence and creativity.

By combining reflective assessment and journaling, your participants will engage in a powerful method to see and accept themselves for who they are, achieve inner strength, and take action to begin viewing themselves more positively.

Thanks to the following professionals for their valuable input in the production of this book.

Amy Brodsky, LISW-S

Carol Butler, MS Ed, RN, C

Kathy Khalsa, MAJS, OTR / L

Jay Leutenberg

Kathy Liptak, Ed.D.

Eileen Regen, M.Ed., CJE

Hannah Lavole

Kally Lavole

For the Facilitator – Enrichment Activities

by Carol Butler, MS Ed, RN, C

Apples and Oranges Questions

Thinking about apples and oranges can help you to avoid comparing yourself with others in your dating relationships, friendships, family, and at school and work. To become all that *you* can be, focus on your *uniqueness*.

Consider apples and oranges: both are fruits, yet different in color, taste, texture, and nutrients. If an orange tried to be an apple by painting itself red, no one would be fooled and the superficial change would not affect the inside. Even within each fruit are different varieties such as McIntosh, Delicious and others.

What do apples and oranges have to do with self-esteem? Much misery is caused by thinking we don't "measure up." The following questions illustrate the futility of comparisons.

1. Name two well-known singers, both popular, but very different.

   _____

   _____

2. Name two popular actors, both talented, but in different ways.

   _____

   _____

3. Name two great athletes, both strong, but in different sports.

   _____

   _____

4. Name two musicians or musical groups, both successful, but in different types of music.

   _____

   _____

5. Consider artists, cartoonists, prose and poetry writers and journalists/TV reporters. Name two who are gifted, but in different ways.

   _____

   _____

(Continued on the next page)

For the Facilitator – Enrichment Activities *(Continued)*

Sometimes comparisons are made by *other people*: parents, teachers, friends, coaches and dating friends.

Tell about a time when you were compared to someone and describe how you felt in the following situations:

1. A parent compared you to a sibling

   _____

   _____

   _____

2. A teacher compared you to a sibling or another student

   _____

   _____

   _____

3. A friend compared you to another friend

   _____

   _____

   _____

4. A coach or Physical Education teacher compared you to someone else

   _____

   _____

   _____

5. A person you dated compared you to someone else

   _____

   _____

   _____

(Continued on the next page)

For the Facilitator – Enrichment Activities *(Continued)*

Describe someone to whom *you* have compared *yourself* and describe how you felt in these situations.

1. In your family _____
   _____

2. At school _____
   _____

3. In a friendship _____
   _____

4. In a dating relationship _____
   _____

5. At work _____
   _____

Consider this situation:

In a dating relationship the guy gawks at a body in a bikini, and his girlfriend is overweight, (or the girl gawks at a muscular man, and her boyfriend is very thin). What would *your* reactions be depending on *your* level of esteem, if your dating friend was the gawker?

Low Esteem Thoughts	High Esteem Thoughts
_____	_____
_____	_____
Low Esteem Feelings	**High Esteem Feelings**
_____	_____
_____	_____
Low Esteem Actions	**High Esteem Actions**
_____	_____
_____	_____
Low Esteem Effects on the Relationship	**High Esteem Effects on the Relationship**
_____	_____
_____	_____

(Continued on the next page)

For the Facilitator – Enrichment Activities (Continued)

The responses below are examples of how some people might have answered the situation, but your answers are best for you because they reflect your personal point of view!

Low Esteem Thoughts: *He thinks I'm fat. She thinks I'm wimpy. I'll be dumped!*

Low Esteem Feelings: *ugly, not good enough, fearful of loss, mad, sad*

Low Esteem Actions: *withdraw with body language, give the silent treatment, make sarcastic remarks, act clingy or domineering, argue, cry, and/or yell*

Low Esteem Effects on the Relationship: *the day at the beach is ruined; eventually the gawker may break up with the date because insecurity is unattractive, or the dating friend may break up with the gawker because of imagining that the gawker no longer cares.*

High Esteem Thoughts: *The person does have a nice body, but I have other attractive qualities, and my date is not with me for my body.*

High Esteem Feelings: *acceptance of own body type, awareness of own attributes*

High Esteem Actions: *Ignore the moment, eat healthy foods and exercise IF being more physically fit is important to me, Tell the gawker, "Please stop."*

High Esteem Effects on the Relationship: *a great day at the beach; if the gawker's behavior continues, the date may decide the relationship is unhealthy and break up because the gawker is too focused on superficial appearance; the date may decide to dump the gawker and find another dating friend who de-emphasizes body build and appreciates more important qualities*

Think about someone who has a quality you truly admire. _____

What can you do to improve yourself in that area? _____

_____

What can you do to improve your different, equally valuable strengths?

_____

What are you now doing to become all that you can be?

_____

Give an example of a situation you are experiencing now, or anticipate in the near future, where you may be tempted to compare yourself with another person.

_____

How will awareness of your individuality help you to avoid comparisons using the "Apples and Oranges" concept.

_____

(Continued on the next page)

For the Facilitator – Enrichment Activities *(Continued)*

Respond to the five quotations from *Desiderata* by Max Ehrmann.

1. *"If you compare yourself with others, you will become bitter or vain, for there will always be greater and lesser persons than yourself."*

   Tell about hanging out with or comparing yourself to someone you perceived to have less (looks, talent, intelligence, etc.) so that you could feel superior.

   _____

   _____

   Do you believe there will always be greater and lesser *persons* than you, or there will always be people with *greater skills* in some ways and *lesser abilities* in other ways?

   _____

   _____

2. *"Be yourself."*

   _____

   _____

3. *"Beyond a wholesome discipline, be gentle with yourself."*

   _____

   _____

4. *"But do not distress yourself with imaginings."*
   Explain how *comparisons* resemble imaginings.

   _____

   _____

5. *"Whatever your labors and aspirations, in the noisy confusion of life, keep pace with your soul."*

   _____

   _____

Introduction for the Participant

Healthy self-esteem is essential for survival and life success. A significant connection between self-esteem and overall life satisfaction is evident. People with healthy self-esteem seem to enjoy life to the fullest, make effective choices to get what they want, connect easily with other people in their lives, trust other people more, and feel at ease expressing emotions and opinions. They are less troubled by inner problems, less affected by the criticism of others, and more adept at finding ways to achieve their full potential. Unhealthy self-esteem can show itself in a variety of ways. Some people with low self-esteem find it difficult to have healthy relationships with others; sometimes they feel depressed, anxious and possibly even worthless.

Self-esteem is your assessment of your personal worth as a human being, and it is largely based on your approval of yourself and the approval of others around you. Because self-esteem is a combination of many traits and attitudes you have about yourself, it can be a challenge to change. Nonetheless, people can change and are able to boost their self-esteem! It happens all the time! You can work to eliminate the causes of low self-esteem and to create a healthy sense of self-esteem.

Self-esteem tends to be a fairly stable quality, but it can swing one way or another based on your relationships, your critical inner thoughts, and the feelings you have about yourself. It's your choice. You can directly build and nourish healthy aspects of your self-esteem and adapt in positive ways to difficult challenges as they occur throughout your life.

CONFIDENTIALITY

The *Teen Self-Esteem Workbook* is designed to provide you with a step-by-step plan to help you build a realistic, healthy, positive sense of self. This approach requires that you learn about yourself by journaling your thoughts and feelings and by practicing the skills that are being taught in this workbook. Therefore, you will be asked to respond to assessments and exercises, and to journal about some experiences in your relationships.

Everyone has the right to confidentiality, and you must honor the right of other people's privacy. Think about it this way – you would not want someone writing things about you that other people could read. Your friends probably feel the same way. In order to maintain the confidentiality of your friends, assign people code names based on things you know about them. For example, a friend named Sherry who loves to wear purple might be coded as *SWP* (Sherry Wears Purple). Do not use any person's actual name when you are listing people.

Teen Self-Esteem Workbook
TABLE OF CONTENTS

TABLE OF CONTENTS

TABLE OF CONTENTS

SECTION I:

Teen Self-Esteem Scale

Name_____

Date_____

Teen Self-Esteem Scale
Directions

Self-esteem is the way you feel about yourself. It is your perception of your worth, as well as your perception of what others think of you. Good self-esteem is being able to think and speak positively and confidently about yourself without bragging or being arrogant. It is one of the most important aspects of your personal development. It is necessary for effective social and emotional growth and is vital in your efforts to reach your full potential.

The *Teen Self-Esteem Scale* can help you identify how you currently feel about yourself. This assessment contains 32 statements. Read each of the statements and decide if the statement is true or false. If it is true, circle the word True next to the statement. If the statement is false, circle the word False next to the statement. Ignore the letters after the True and False choices. They are for scoring purposes and will be used later. Complete all 32 items before going back to score the Self-Esteem Scale.

In the following example, the circled False indicates that the item is false for the person completing the scale:

1. I need constant approval and recognition. . . . . True (B) (False (A)) Score _____

This is not a test and there are no right or wrong answers. Do not spend too much time thinking about your answers. Your initial response will be the most true for you. Be sure to respond to every statement.

(Turn to the next page and begin)

Teen Self-Esteem Scale

1. I need constant approval and recognition . . . . True (B)   False (A)   Score _____

2. I am often embarrassed by the actions of others . . . . . True (B)   False (A)   Score _____

3. I am concerned about what others think of me. . . . . . True (B)   False (A)   Score _____

4. I am hurt by the opinions and comments of others. . . True (B)   False (A)   Score _____

5. I give in to other people quickly. . . . . True (B)   False (A)   Score _____

6. I am judgmental of others. True (B)   False (A)   Score _____

7. I openly voice my opinions . . . . True (A)   False (B)   Score _____

8. Even if I don't want to, I often go along
   with the crowd. . . . . True (B)   False (A)   Score _____

I. TOTAL = _____

9. It doesn't bother me to talk in front of
   a group of people. . . . . True (A)   False (B)   Score _____

10. I rarely know how to start a conversation. . . . . True (B)   False (A)   Score _____

11. I often feel inadequate in a new situation . . . . True (B)   False (A)   Score _____

12. I am shy when I am with other people. . . . . True (B)   False (A)   Score _____

13. Big crowds make me nervous . . . . True (B)   False (A)   Score _____

13. I am friendly and comfortable with new people . . . . . True (A)   False (B)   Score _____

14. I like new and different situations. . . . . True (A)   False (B)   Score _____

16. I don't like to be with other people . . . . True (B)   False (A)   Score _____

II. TOTAL = _____

(Continued on the next page)

(Teen Self-Esteem Scale continued)

17. I don't think I'm anyone special. .... True (B)   False (A)   Score _____

18. I often say I should have .... True (B)   False (A)   Score _____

19. I am able to evaluate what is good about me. .... True (A)   False (B)   Score _____

20. I have a high opinion of myself .... True (A)   False (B)   Score _____

21. I can figure out what I need to improve
    about myself. .... True (A)   False (B)   Score _____

22. I don't often speak my mind, even if I know
    I'm right. .... True (B)   False (A)   Score _____

23. I am proud of myself .... True (A)   False (B)   Score _____

24. I often feel like a loser. .... True (B)   False (A)   Score _____

III. TOTAL = _____

25. I often exaggerate the truth in order to maintain
    my image .... True (B)   False (A)   Score _____

26. I don't feel ashamed of myself. .... True (A)   False (B)   Score _____

27. I often wish I had what other people have .... True (B)   False (A)   Score _____

28. I make excuses when I make mistakes. .... True (B)   False (A)   Score _____

29. It is most important to me to do what
    I think is right .... True (A)   False (B)   Score _____

30. I feel that I look as good as most people. .... True (A)   False (B)   Score _____

31. I would not change much about myself .... True (A)   False (B)   Score _____

32. I often brag about myself and
    my accomplishments .... True (A)   False (B)   Score _____

IV. TOTAL = _____

(Go to the Scoring Directions on the next page)

Teen Self-Esteem Scale
Scoring Directions

The *Teen Self-Esteem Scale* is designed to help you better understand your level of self-esteem. This assessment will help assist you in getting to know yourself better and provide you with insights into your perceptions of yourself. People with high self-esteem consider themselves worthy and view themselves as equal to others. They do not think that they are perfect, but they recognize their limitations and are continually striving to grow and improve.

Scoring the Assessment

Look at the 32 items. Now you need to focus on the **A** and **B** after each choice rather than the True or False. In the space marked Score for each item, award yourself one (1) point for every answer you circled with an **A** next to it and zero (0) points for every answer you circled with a **B** next to it. Then total your score on all items and write that number in the blank below:

    I. Approval Total _____

    II. Social Total _____

    III. Pride Total _____

    IV. Image Total _____

Turn to the next page to interpret your scores on the Teen Self-Esteem Scale.

Teen Self-Esteem Scale
Profile Interpretation

Individual Scale Score	Result	Indications
0 to 2	low	You seem to possess few of the characteristics of someone who has healthy self-esteem. You need to develop skills to respect yourself, consider yourself worthy, and begin to move directly and realistically toward your personal and future goals.
3 to 5	moderate	You possess some of the characteristics of someone who has healthy self-esteem. You seem to respect yourself, consider yourself worthy, and show that you are able to move directly and realistically toward your personal and future goals.
6 to 8	high	You possess many of the characteristics of someone who has healthy self-esteem. You respect yourself, consider yourself worthy, and you are able to move directly and realistically toward your personal and future goals.

For scales you scored in the **Moderate** or **High** range, find the descriptions on the pages that follow. Then, read the description and complete the exercises that follow. No matter how you scored, low, moderate or high, you will benefit from every one of these exercises that are designed to help you to increase your understanding of your level of self-esteem.

Scale Descriptions

APPROVAL – High scores indicate that you do not necessarily need the approval and recognition of others, you are concerned about what others think of you but do not obsess over their comments, and you are not easily influenced by what others do.

SOCIAL – High scores indicate that you enjoy and feel at ease when meeting other people for the first time, you feel comfortable in new situations, and you enjoy being in social situations where you can be with other people.

PRIDE – High scores indicate that you take pride in yourself and your accomplishments, hold yourself in high regard, and know what your strengths are and work to improve on those aspects that you feel are your weaknesses.

IMAGE – High scores indicate that you have a strong self-image, are comfortable with the way you are on the inside and look on the outside, and are not overly concerned about projecting an untrue self-image.

In the following exercises, remember to use Name Codes for the people you describe.

Approval

Think about why you need the approval of other people to make yourself feel better. In the following table, list the people whose approval you need, and why you feel you need it. Use name codes.

People Whose Approval I Think I Need	Why I Need Their Approval

What surprises did you discover in your responses?

_____

_____

Social Situations

Think about the social situations that block your self-esteem. In the following table, identify the social situations you fear and why they are so uncomfortable for you. Use name codes.

Situations That Block My Self-Esteem	Why Is It Uncomfortable for Me?

What surprises did you discover in your responses?

_____

_____

My Pride

List what you are proud of that you do exceptionally well:

_____

_____

_____

_____

_____

_____

_____

_____

List what you are proud of that you do pretty well:

_____

_____

_____

_____

_____

_____

_____

_____

List what you don't do very well but would like to work at doing better:

_____

_____

_____

_____

_____

_____

_____

_____

I am Proud of Me

Finish these sentence starters about what you are most proud of in your life.

My successes at school _____

_____.

With my creative powers _____

_____.

In my spare time I achieve _____

_____.

In athletics I have accomplished _____

_____.

In my community I have _____

_____.

As a volunteer I have I been responsible for_____

_____.

To earn money, I _____

_____.

To help the environment, I _____

_____.

For my neighbors, I have _____

_____.

Other _____

_____.

Image

When you become an adult, what would you like to be known for? Why?

_____

_____

_____

_____

_____

What are some positive ways you have helped other people?

_____

_____

_____

_____

_____

What are some positive ways you have supported yourself?

_____

_____

_____

_____

_____

What is one thing you like to do, that you do very well?

_____

_____

_____

_____

_____

How I Like Myself

What is it about you that you like? Take your time and think about all of the different things you like about yourself. Examples might include *I play violin well*, *I like my style of writing*, *I am a nice person*, and *I like to play chess and am a good sport if I lose.*

Write, draw or doodle what you like about yourself below.

Positive Influencers on Your Self-Esteem

Think about the people who positively influence your self-esteem. In the following table, identify the people who positively influence your self-esteem and how they are able to do so. Use name codes.

People Who Positively Influence My Self-Esteem	How They Do So

Negative Influencers on Your Self-Esteem

Think about the people who negatively influence your self-esteem. In the following table, identify the people who negatively influence your self-esteem and how they are able to do so.

People Who Negatively Influence My Self-Esteem	How They Are Able to Do So

Top 3 about Me!

I am good at . . .

1. _____
2. _____
3. _____

I find it easy to . . .

1. _____
2. _____
3. _____

I am not . . .

1. _____
2. _____
3. _____

I like to . . .

1. _____
2. _____
3. _____

I wish that . . .

1. _____
2. _____
3. _____

Positive Self-Esteem Affirmations

Positive affirmations work! An affirmation can help you replace a negative thought with a more helpful positive one. By using and repeating positive affirmations you can train your brain to think in positive ways: using positive self-talk can change how you feel and think about any situation and yourself. Being positive is very important. It will help you become more successful in everything you do, and your self esteem will increase!

Cut these affirmations and keep them handy in obvious places so they are available to read at any time.

I am open to change.	I feel confident.
I deserve to be liked.	It is okay to have done my best.
I have the right to be heard.	I am valuable.
I have the power to change.	I can own my strengths.
I can make good decisions.	I am capable of learning.

Feedback and Approval

In what situations do you need feedback and/or approval from others?

_____

_____

_____

_____

_____

_____

_____

_____

_____

_____

Who in your life do you feel you must ask for feedback and seek approval? (Use name codes.) Why?

_____

_____

_____

_____

_____

_____

_____

_____

_____

_____

_____

Situations I Find Myself In

In which situations do you feel most uncomfortable?

_____

_____

_____

_____

_____

In which do you feel most comfortable?

_____

_____

_____

_____

_____

In which situations do you feel not good enough?

_____

_____

_____

_____

_____

In which situations do you feel absolutely as good as anyone else?

_____

_____

_____

_____

_____

Spending time in a comfortable situation is great – and – working on being okay in ANY situation is something to strive for!

People with Healthy Self-Esteem...

- face daily events with optimism and a positive outlook

- take better care of their emotional, mental and physical health

- overcome adversity and setbacks more easily

- persevere when facing obstacles

- live according to their values

- accept themselves more easily

- live in the present

- see the good in others and in themselves

- take responsibility for their thoughts, feelings and actions

- feel confident without boasting or being arrogant

- accept constructive criticism

- remain calm and thoughtful when facing setbacks

- can laugh at themselves and not take themselves too seriously

- communicate in an assertive way

- learn from their mistakes

- avoid blaming

- avoid making excuses

- avoid putting down others

Unhealthy Comments Indicate Low Self-Esteem

- "I can't be happy unless I have... (money, success, love, approval, etc.)"

- "I am not good enough"

- "Life is harder for me than for anyone else"

- "If people criticize me, I'm no good"

- "Life isn't fair"

- "I deserve to have what other people have"

- "I must be liked by everyone or I'm not okay"

- "I need to be competent at everything"

- "I must stay busy to be worthy"

- "I am nothing"

- "There is something wrong with me"

- "I am a terrible person"

- "I just have bad luck!"

SECTION II:

Teen Self-Worth Scale

Name_____

Date_____

Teen Self-Worth Scale
Directions

Self-worth refers to the notion that you are an important and valuable person because of who you are. Self-worth implies that you are as worthy a person as anyone else. Self-worth is what you are born with – you are worthwhile and have value. It cannot be taken from you, but it is possible that you can lose sight of it. Your self-worth now is what you perceive it to be and how you believe you are doing in your world in terms of skills, achievement, personality, etc. The *Teen Self-Worth Scale* is designed to help you begin this self-reflection process.

This assessment contains 28 statements related to your self-worth. Read each of the statements and decide whether or not the statement describes you. If the statement *does* describe you, circle the number in the YES column. If the statement *does not* describe you, circle the number in the NO column.

In the following example, the circled number under YES indicates the statement is descriptive of the person completing the inventory.

	YES	NO
I constantly criticize myself.	(1)	2

This is not a test and there are no right or wrong answers. Do not spend too much time thinking about your answers. Your initial response will be the most true for you.
Be sure to respond to every statement.

(Turn to the next page and begin)

Teen Self-Worth Scale

	YES	NO
I constantly criticize myself	1	2
I have many positive skills and qualities	2	1
I accept the fact that I'm not perfect	2	1
I take care of myself	2	1
I understand how I am special	2	1
I have a hard time accepting and liking myself	1	2
I often compare myself to others with envy	1	2

A - TOTAL _____

I like how I look and behave physically	2	1
I feel jealous of people with great bodies	1	2
I think people put too much value on someone's looks	2	1
My weight is a constant issue with me	1	2
I am not comfortable with my body	1	2
I do not worry about my body being adequate enough	2	1
I hate to look in a full length mirror	1	2

B - TOTAL _____

(Continued on the next page)

(Teen Self-Worth Scale continued)

	YES	NO
I usually see the glass half full	2	1
I worry about things beyond my control.	1	2
I usually look at the bright side of things	2	1
I am not a positive person	1	2
My first reaction is I can't or it can't be done	1	2
I relive my mistakes over and over	1	2
I see success in my future.	2	1

P - TOTAL _____

I worry excessively about what other people say about me	1	2
I feel rejected when others don't pay attention to me.	1	2
I compare myself favorably to others	2	1
My personal self-worth is based on opinions others have of me	1	2
It is vital to me that every single person likes or accepts me	1	2
I'm not sure I've done a good job until someone tells me so	1	2
My own opinions count more to me than strangers' opinions	2	1

S - TOTAL _____

(Go to the Scoring Directions on the next page)

Teen Self-Worth Scale
Scoring Directions

The *Teen Self-Worth Scale* is designed to help you explore various aspects of your perceived self-worth - how you view yourself. On the previous two pages, add the numbers that you circled in each section and write the scores on each of the TOTAL lines. You will receive a total in the range from 7 to 14. Then, transfer those numbers to the spaces below.

A = Self-Acceptance   **Total** = _____

B = Body Image   **Total** = _____

P = Positive Outlook   **Total** = _____

S = Self-Approval   **Total** = _____

Profile Interpretation

Individual Scale Score	Result	Indications
7 to 9	low	You have a limited perceived belief in your own self-worth. It is important for you to develop a better image of yourself, accept yourself as you are and who you can become, maintain a positive view of life, and not rely completely on the opinions of others.
10 to 11	moderate	You have a fairly healthy belief in your own self-worth. It is important for you to develop an even better image of yourself, accept yourself as you are and who you can become, maintain a positive view of life, and not rely too heavily on the opinions of others.
12 to 14	high	You have a very healthy belief in your own self-worth. It is important for you to continue to develop your image of yourself, accept yourself as you are and who you can become, maintain a positive view of life, and not rely very much on the opinions of others.

No matter how you scored on the Teen Self-Worth Scale (Low, Moderate or High), you will benefit from doing all of the following exercises.

Teen Self-Worth
Scale Descriptions

Self-Acceptance

People scoring high on this scale tend to accept themselves for who they are, accepting their imperfections as well as their positive qualities. They are not overly self-critical and when they believe they need to improve themselves, they do this in positive ways. They are committed to lifelong growth and improvement.

Body Image

People scoring high on this scale feel confident and comfortable in their own body and do not spend an unreasonable amount of time being concerned about weight, height, etc. They understand that a person's physical appearance says very little about the character, self-worth or value as a person. They are committed to keeping their body as healthy as possible.

Positive Outlook

People scoring high on this scale have an outlook on life that is generally upbeat and positive. They see the brighter, optimistic viewpoints, tend not to blame themselves too much, persevere through setbacks and obstacles, and find joy in the small things in life. They take the opportunity to learn from their mistakes and look upon them as valuable life lessons.

Self-Approval

People scoring high on this scale do what they believe to be right for them, behaving according to their values, as well as what is right for the greater good. They will listen to the opinions of others and consider them in their decision making, but they do not make value judgments about themselves based on these opinions. They realize that there is no connection between their personal worth and how people feel about them.

Your Perception of Your Self-Worth

Your self-worth is your general mental picture of your value as a person. Your self-worth is how you see yourself and includes many different types of factors including what you think you look like, what kind of person you think you are, how you view life, and what you believe others think of you. Self-worth, then, has to do with perception. How you see yourself definitely affects how you act, think, and relate to other people. Your self-worth is tied to self-esteem because the higher your self-esteem, the more positively you will see yourself. The lower your self-esteem, the more critical of yourself you will tend to be.

Remember that your feelings and perceptions of your self-worth can be very different from how the world sees you. Some people appear to have a great sense of self-worth and have led a very difficult life. On the other hand, some people have a low sense of self-worth even though they are very successful.

It is important that your self-worth is positive and realistic. Many factors affect the realistic nature of your self-worth.

Sample factors:

- Listening to your internal, often critical voice

- Allowing another's opinions of you to become more important than your own realistic opinion of yourself

- Emphasizing the negative, rather than the positive, in most situations

- Feeling guilty about things beyond your control

- Focusing on your weaknesses rather than your strengths

Now that you have identified some of the factors affecting your self-worth, you can make a definite effort to realistically look at your perceptions of yourself. Complete all of the exercises and activities that follow.

What I Like about My Body

Think about those aspects of your body that you like most.

What I Like about My Body	Why

What I Dislike about My Body

Think about those aspects of your body that you dislike most.

What I Dislike about My Body	Why	If It Is Under My Control, How Can I Change It?

My Body Image

What is under your control to help you accept your body?

_____

_____

_____

What is not under your control to help you accept your body? How can you let it go?

_____

_____

_____

To whom do you compare yourself when it comes to your body image? (name codes)

_____

_____

_____

Describe how your body is unique.

_____

_____

_____

What would you never want to change about your body?

_____

_____

_____

Do you think there might be things about your body that you don't like now, but you might as an adult?

_____

_____

_____

Self-Acceptance

Think about the things you like most about yourself. These aspects could be related to school, work, friends, family, community, etc. They could include skills, abilities, personality traits, interpersonal skills. Complete the following exercise to explore the things you like most about yourself.

What I Like About Myself	Why I Like It
My Personality	
Myself as a Friend	
Myself as a Family Member	
My Mind	
My Body	
My Values	
My Confidence	
My Caring	

I Am Proud of Myself

Personality traits I possess that I am most proud of _____

_____

_____

_____

Accomplishments I am most proud of _____

_____

_____

_____

Skills I possess that make me proud are _____

_____

_____

_____

Goals I set and am working to achieved are _____

_____

_____

_____

Values I hold that I am most proud of are _____

_____

_____

_____

Qualities, characteristics and traits I possess that I am most proud of are _____

_____

_____

_____

My Negative Thoughts

You have many thoughts streaming through your mind. Some of these will be positive but some will be negative. These negative thoughts can change your attitude and therefore lower your self-esteem. The following activity is designed to help you recognize and change those negative thoughts.

My Negative Thoughts	How I Can Reverse Them to Positive
School *Ex: I'll never finish my homework today.*	*If I hurry home, skip TV, go on the internet for 10 minutes only, I can get it done!*
School	
Home	
Friends	
The environment	
Family	
My body	
My attitude	
The government	

Working on Yourself!

Positive and negative thinking can be contagious. (Use name codes)

Which of your friends are positive thinkers?

_____

_____

_____

_____

Which of your friends are negative thinkers?
How do they influence you? What can you do about that?

_____

_____

_____

_____

All people have flaws.
What are two or three of your major flaws and how can you work on them?
In what ways are you hard on yourself?

_____

_____

_____

_____

Avoid exaggerating in order to be credible in your relationships.
About what or whom do you tend to exaggerate?

_____

_____

_____

_____

Others' Opinions of Me

Often we behave in ways in order to gain approval from others, in order to be liked or even loved, to prove ourselves, to be accepted, or because of our fear of rejection. It is important to sort out whether others opinions are beneficial to you or not.

Others' Opinions (Use Name Codes)	True or Not?	To React or Ignore. Why?
Ex: My friend JM says I was a coward when I saw someone being bullied and I just stood by.	Yes	Next time, I will leave and go for help. This person was hurt and maybe I could have made a difference.

Self-Approval vs. Others' Opinions

Whose opinions matter most to you? Use name codes.

_____

_____

_____

_____

Are their opinions for your benefit or theirs?

_____

_____

_____

_____

What do you do that others want you to, but that you don't feel may be best?

_____

_____

_____

_____

What do you not do that others want you to, because you know it's not a good idea?

_____

_____

_____

_____

How can you hear peoples' opinions and then move on to do what you feel is right?

_____

_____

_____

_____

Self-Worth Quotes

These quotes are related to how worthy you perceive yourself to be as an individual. Choose the one that speaks to you and write a short story related to the quote about something that happened in your life.

❑ *If I am not for myself, who will be?* ~ **Hillel**

❑ *Self-worth comes from one thing – thinking that you are worthy.* ~ **Wayne Dyer**

❑ *Through self-doubt we lose our sense of self-worth.* ~ **Author unknown**

❑ *When you are a beautiful person on the inside, there is nothing in the world that can change that about you. Jealousy is the result of one's lack of self-confidence, self-worth and self-acceptance. The lesson: If you can't accept yourself, then certainly no one else will.*
~ *Sasha Azeredo*

_____

_____

_____

_____

_____

_____

_____

_____

_____

_____

_____

_____

_____

_____

_____

_____

_____

_____

_____

_____

_____

Self-Acceptance

Journal some of your feelings about yourself.

_____

_____

_____

_____

_____

_____

_____

_____

_____

_____

_____

_____

_____

_____

_____

_____

_____

_____

_____

_____

_____

_____

_____

_____

_____

_____

_____

What Can You Do?

Journal about what you can do to improve your observations about yourself if you see any that you feel need improving.

_____

_____

_____

_____

_____

_____

_____

_____

_____

_____

_____

_____

_____

_____

_____

_____

_____

_____

_____

_____

_____

_____

_____

_____

_____

_____

_____

_____

Your Self-Worth Includes these Aspects:

- What you think about yourself

- What you think you look like

- What kind of person you think you are

- How you view the world

- How much you like yourself

- How much you think others like you

- Your opinion of yourself

- Your attitude as you go through life

- How you present yourself to yourself and others

Other Ways to Improve Self-Worth

- Change negative thoughts to positive ones

- Accept compliments gracefully

- Continually question the negative views you have of yourself

- Accept criticism as constructive suggestions and then move on

- Don't be so hard on yourself

- Set realistic and attainable goals

- Stop comparing yourself to others

- Give yourself positive affirmations

- Continue to develop your strengths

- Be with people who have positive attitudes

SECTION III:

Teen Self-Assertiveness Scale

Name_____

Date_____

Teen Assertiveness Scale
Directions

Assertiveness means standing up for your rights while being careful not to intrude on the rights of others. It is expressing your personal wants and needs, following your interests and personal likes, easily giving and accepting compliments, comfortably disagreeing with others, learning to say no when you do not want to do something, and protecting yourself when something seems unfair.

By learning to be more assertive, you will be able to get what you need and desire without being aggressive or passive. All people have a right to express their feelings, thoughts, and opinions; the right to expect others not to criticize them harshly; and the expectation that others will treat them with respect. In your friendships and other relationships, you respond in one of three ways: passively, assertively or aggressively.

The Teen Assertiveness Scale contains 33 statements. Read each of the statements and decide the extent to which the statement describes you. In each of the choices listed, circle the number of your response on the line to the right of each statement.

In the following example, the circled 4 indicates the statement is very much like the person completing the inventory:

4 = Very Much Like Me	3 = Usually Like Me	2 = Somewhat Like Me	1 = Not Like Me

1. I say nothing when others provoke me. . . . . (4) 3 2 1

This is not a test and there are no right or wrong answers. Do not spend too much time thinking about your answers. Your initial response will be the most true for you.
Be sure to respond to every statement.

(Turn to the next page and begin)

Teen Assertiveness Scale

4 = Very Much Like Me	3 = Usually Like Me	2 = Somewhat Like Me	1 = Not Like Me

1. I say nothing when others provoke me. 4   3   2   1

2. I react to other people who are aggressive. 4   3   2   1

3. I express my thoughts and feelings directly to others 4   3   2   1

4. I keep my feelings to myself. 4   3   2   1

5. I do not mind if I hurt other people by being unkind. 4   3   2   1

6. I am honest with other people 4   3   2   1

7. I hide my feelings from significant others. 4   3   2   1

8. I express my feelings through insults and put-downs 4   3   2   1

9. I treat others with respect and dignity 4   3   2   1

10. I let other people violate my personal rights 4   3   2   1

11. I can be very sarcastic. 4   3   2   1

12. I do not feel guilty when I act firmly and confidently in my own best interest 4   3   2   1

13. I let others bully me 4   3   2   1

14. I often label other people. 4   3   2   1

15. I stand up for myself without 4   3   2   1

16. I let others take advantage of me. 4   3   2   1

17. I often treat people disrespectfully. 4   3   2   1

(Continued on the next page)

(Teen Assertiveness Scale continued)

4 = Very Much Like Me	3 = Usually Like Me	2 = Somewhat Like Me	1 = Not Like Me

	4	3	2	1
18. I try not to hurt others when reaching for what I want.	4	3	2	1
19. I do things I do not want to do	4	3	2	1
20. I force others to do things they do not want to do	4	3	2	1
21. I defend others who cannot stick up for themselves	4	3	2	1
22. I let other people treat me disrespectfully	4	3	2	1
23. I don't care about the feelings of others.	4	3	2	1
24. I constantly search for all around positive solutions to problems	4	3	2	1
25. I often think that my ideas are worthless	4	3	2	1
26. I often bully or intimidate others.	4	3	2	1
27. I often hold my ground and search for compromises	4	3	2	1
28. I constantly apologize for my behavior.	4	3	2	1
29. I try to force people to change their minds	4	3	2	1
30. I recognize my own and others' rights	4	3	2	1
31. I give in to others and then I don't feel good about myself.	4	3	2	1
32. I make others feel guilty so I can get my way.	4	3	2	1
33. Others may not agree with me but they still respect my opinion.	4	3	2	1

(Go to the Scoring Directions on the next page)

Teen Assertiveness Scale
Scoring Directions

Teens are being asked to stand up for their rights and the rights of others more often than in the past. Passive people are unable to stand up for their rights and they give in to others. Aggressive people are demanding and inconsiderate. Assertive people are able to express personal feelings and rights in an honest, open and direct way.

The *Teen Assertiveness Scale* is designed to measure the level of your assertiveness in attaining what you want and need in life. Three areas have been identified to make up the scales: Passive, Aggressive and Assertive.

Items that comprise each of the three scales are grouped so that you can explore how assertively you behave.

To score the assessment:

1) Record each of the scores from the previous two pages on the lines below. For example, if you circled the 4 for item number 1, you would put a 4 on the line above the 1 on the chart below. Do the same for all 33 items.

2) Add the totals for each of the 3 rows and put that total on the total line to the right.

1	4	7	10	13	16	19	22	25	28	31	Passive Total
2	5	8	11	14	17	20	23	26	29	32	Aggressive Total
3	6	9	12	15	18	21	24	27	30	33	Assertive Total

Teen Assertiveness Scale
Profile Interpretation

Total Scores for Each of the Scales	Result	Indications
33 to 44	high	You will often use this assertiveness style when communicating your wants and needs.
22 to 32	moderate	You will sometimes use this assertiveness style when communicating your wants and needs.
11 to 21	low	You will not often use this often this assertiveness style when communicating your wants and needs.

The scale on which you scored the highest represents your style in communicating what you want or need. The remainder of the assessment contains exercises to help determine how assertively you act. The scale will help you to identify whether your actions are passive, aggressive or assertive in nature.

The following sections will provide a description of the three behaviors as well as some self-reflective questions to help you become more assertive.

Scale Descriptions

Passive – You are non-assertive and express your wants, needs, opinions and feelings in an indirect manner. You might cry, pout, yawn or become angry at yourself, all the while keeping your feelings inside. You expect others to know what you want and how you feel. Your needs come after the needs of everyone else. You have trouble saying no and asking for what you want. You may have trouble making eye contact with other people. You let other people violate your personal rights to be treated with respect and dignity.

Aggressive – You have no trouble expressing your wants, opinions and feelings, but often do so at the expense of others. You use sarcasm and put-downs as a way of controlling other people. You like to get your own way and will do anything to do so. You often hurt others by your verbal, nonverbal and physical behavior. You tend to infringe on the rights of others by expressing your feelings indirectly through labels, insults, and hostile statements. You tend to express your thoughts, feelings, and opinions in a way that violates other peoples' right to be treated with respect and dignity.

Assertive – You tend to take other peoples' rights and feelings into account when you express your wants, needs, opinions and feelings. Because you are able to defend yourself by using many *I-statements*, you listen to others and let them know that you understand their points of view. You tend to know what you want, ask for what you want, and set limits about how you let others treat you. You receive and give compliments easily, listen carefully and respond well to constructive feedback from others.

Unhealthy Relationships – Part 1

Some relationships help you feel good about yourself and your personal goals. Other relationships are damaging to you and to your self-esteem. Think about your current relationships. Below, list the people who are unhealthy for your self-esteem and how they damage your self-esteem. Use name codes.

People Unhealthy for My Self-Esteem	How They Damage My Self-Esteem
Ex: JKF	He uses pressure to get me to do things I don't want, but I want to be part of his crowd.

Unhealthy Relationships – Part 2

List the people from Part 1, on the previous page. Which relationships are worth saving? Describe how you can assertively communicate how your friendship needs to change so that you can feel better about it and yourself.

People Unhealthy for My Self-Esteem	Ways I Can Assertively Change the Relationship for the Better
Ex: JKF	*He uses pressure to get me to do things I don't want, but I want to be part of his crowd.*

Lack of Assertiveness

Describe ways your lack of assertiveness caused problems for you.

My friends _____
_____
_____
_____

My social life _____
_____
_____
_____

My job _____
_____
_____
_____

My volunteering _____
_____
_____
_____

My possessions _____
_____
_____
_____

My family _____
_____
_____
_____

(Continued on the next page)

Lack of Assertiveness *(Continued)*

Other ways I have had problems by not being assertive are _____

_____

_____

_____

_____

_____

_____

_____

_____

_____

_____

_____

_____

_____

When I don't stand up for myself, I feel _____

_____

_____

_____

_____

_____

_____

_____

_____

_____

_____

_____

_____

Once, When I Was Assertive ...

_____
_____
_____
_____
_____
_____

(Above, write about a time when you were assertive.)

I liked _____
_____
_____
_____
_____

It was difficult to _____
_____
_____
_____
_____

As I look back, I could have said or done _____
_____
_____
_____
_____

From the experience, I gained _____
_____
_____
_____

My Priorities

To assert yourself, you must know what you want. By establishing priorities, you will be able to assert yourself when you need to. You will know what is worth pursuing and will be aware of the things you want to walk away from, or put on hold for the future. In each of the boxes below, list your priorities in each of the categories. Use name codes.

	My Priorities
Example: Personal	*I want to be talked to and treated with the same respect I give to others.*
Personal	
School Friends	
School Authorities	
Family	
Friends	
Dating Relationships	
Religiously/Spiritually	
Work/Volunteer	
Community	
By People in General	
Other	
Other	

Irrational Thoughts about Assertiveness

A lack of assertiveness often stems from irrational thoughts you have about yourself and the way the world operates. The following chart includes ten irrational thoughts that cause people to be less assertive. Next to the irrational thought that is listed, identify the reasons if and why you often have that irrational thought. Use name codes.

Irrational Thoughts	Why I Think That
Don't rock the boat, just go along with the crowd.	
Put others' needs before your own.	
Never make mistakes.	
Always accommodate other people before yourself.	
Be sensitive to the needs of others, not your own.	
Stay on other people's good side at all times.	
You should respect the view of people in authority.	
It is never polite to question the views of others.	
Keep your opinions to yourself.	
Asking questions shows your ignorance.	
Other	

Non-Assertive Situations

To become more assertive, it will be helpful to be aware of those situations in which you are not assertive. For each of the situations listed below, describe how you show a lack of assertiveness.

Situations in Which I Lack Assertiveness	Why I Am Non-Assertive
Ex: *Saying* No *to others*	*I feel guilty and I worry that I won't be accepted.*
Saying *No* to others	
Disagreeing with others' opinions	
Taking charge of a situation	
Social situations	
Letting someone know what I want	
Stating my opinion	
Asking for help	
Pressure from peers	
Finding time by myself	
Speaking in front of groups	
Others	

People with Whom I am Not Very Assertive

By identifying those people with whom you are not assertive, you can later practice your assertive skills with them. For each of the people listed below, describe how you show a lack of assertiveness. Use name codes.

People with Whom I am Passive	Why I am Passive
Ex: Family Member - GMB	I am afraid GMB will hurt me or ground me.
Family member	
Dating friend	
People at work	
Friends	
School authorities	
Neighbors	
People in my community	
Kids at parties	
Large groups	
Others	

Ways I Can Respond Assertively

In your own words, define assertiveness.

_____

_____

_____

How can you respond to the situations below in an assertive way?

Write your response and/or role-play with another person.

- *Your teacher accused you of cheating. You didn't.*

_____

_____

_____

- *A family member told you that you can't watch a TV show required by your teacher.*

_____

_____

_____

- *Your friend reminded you of a favor she had done for you once and wanted you to do something you didn't approve of.*

_____

_____

_____

- *You saved and saved for an I-Pod and it doesn't work right. You need to take it back.*

_____

_____

_____

- *Your grandmother always talks very softly to you from across the room and you can't hear her.*

_____

_____

_____

- *You strongly disagree with a friend who is speaking out passionately about a political issue.*

_____

_____

_____

Assertiveness Quotations

Check a quote that at first reading seems a little difficult to understand. Write about what you think it means, and then talk with some people and discuss your interpretation.

❑ *Assertiveness is not what you do, it's who you are.*
~ Cal Le Mon

❑ *The basic difference between being assertive and being aggressive is how our words and behavior affect the rights and well-being of others.*
~ Sharon Anthony Bower

❑ *There is a fine line between assertiveness and being relaxed.*
~ Justin Guarini

_____

_____

_____

_____

_____

_____

_____

_____

_____

_____

_____

_____

_____

_____

_____

_____

_____

_____

_____

_____

_____

_____

© 2011 WHOLE PERSON ASSOCIATES, 210 WEST MICHIGAN ST., DULUTH MN 55802-1908 ▪ 800-247-6789

The New Assertive Me

Write a letter to yourself, explaining how you will begin to act more assertively, with whom (use name codes), and in which situations. Keep the letter handy, reading it every day for two weeks. Make progress notes on the back of the page. You can do it!

Dear _____,

_____

_____

_____

_____

_____

_____

_____

_____

_____

_____

_____

_____

_____

_____

_____

_____

_____

_____

_____

_____

_____

_____

_____

Signed _____

Non-Verbal Communication

When acting assertively I should remember:

1) Maintain a positive, assertive body posture

2) Relax

3) Express myself in an honest, open and direct way

4) Maintain good eye-contact

5) Maintain a normal conversational distance

6) Keep my voice warm and my tone calm

7) Adopt a pleasant facial expression

8) Listen carefully

Practice this behavior with a partner

Assertiveness Checklist

Things to remember about being assertive:

- I decide for myself what I will and will not do.

- I will not be influenced by peer pressure.

- I do not have to defend myself to others.

- The feedback of others cannot hurt me but it might help me.

- It is okay to ask for what I want and need.

- My opinion counts.

- Everyone does not have to like my opinion.

- I am not responsible for others' problems.

- I have the right to ask for help.

- I can make my own decisions.

- I am in charge of my own behavior.

SECTION IV:

Teen Self-Understanding Scale

Name_____

Date_____

Teen Self-Understanding Scale
Directions

Self-understanding is an awareness of who you are and what makes you special.

This awareness includes understanding ...

- Your uniqueness

- Your personality

- Your purpose in life

- Your emotional triggers

This assessment contains forty statements. Read each of the statements and circle the number to the right of the statement that describes your level of awareness.

In the following example, the circled number 2 indicates that the participant completing the scale is fairly aware of the feelings he or she experiences the most:

	Very Aware	Fairly Aware	Not Very Aware

I am aware of...

1. the feelings I experience most...................... 3   (2)   1

This is not a test and there are no right or wrong answers. Do not spend too much time thinking about your answers. Your initial response will be the most true for you. Be sure to respond to every statement.

(Turn to the next page and begin)

Teen Self-Understanding Scale

	Very Aware	Fairly Aware	Not Very Aware
I am aware of ...			
1. the feelings I experience most	3	2	1
2. how I hold in my feelings	3	2	1
3. how my emotions affect other people	3	2	1
4. the situations in which I get too emotional	3	2	1
5. how my emotions affect my behavior	3	2	1
6. which emotions both help and hurt me	3	2	1
7. how my emotions affect my thinking	3	2	1
8. how my emotions can help me to better understand situations	3	2	1
9. when I overreact because of how I am feeling	3	2	1
10. what makes me happy	3	2	1

I. TOTAL _____

	Very Aware	Fairly Aware	Not Very Aware
I am aware of ...			
11. my personal limitations	3	2	1
12. my sense of humor	3	2	1
13. my abilities	3	2	1
14. how I learn best	3	2	1
15. my talents	3	2	1
16. my strengths	3	2	1
17. my weaknesses	3	2	1
18. how I am special	3	2	1
19. what I am good at	3	2	1
20. how much I have yet to learn	3	2	1

II. TOTAL _____

(Continued on the next page)

(Teen Self-Understanding Scale continued)

I am aware of ...	Very Aware	Fairly Aware	Not Very Aware
21. what brings me happiness	3	2	1
22. my particular personality	3	2	1
23. what helps me feel peaceful	3	2	1
24. what frustrates me	3	2	1
25. what makes me laugh	3	2	1
26. what triggers my anger	3	2	1
27. what excites me	3	2	1
28. when I become sad	3	2	1
29. where I feel most comfortable	3	2	1
30. in what situation I become impatient	3	2	1

III. TOTAL _____

I am aware of ...	Very Aware	Fairly Aware	Not Very Aware
31. my intolerant ideas / feelings	3	2	1
32. what makes me special	3	2	1
33. what I want to know more about	3	2	1
34. what I look forward to as an adult	3	2	1
35. what brings me the greatest joy	3	2	1
36. what I do better than many people	3	2	1
37. what I value the most	3	2	1
38. how I would like to make a difference	3	2	1
39. what I might want to do with my life	3	2	1
40. what I feel passionate about	3	2	1

IV. TOTAL _____

(Go to the Scoring Directions on the next page)

Teen Self-Understanding Scale Scoring Directions

The Self-Understanding Scale is designed to help you to explore your awareness of your emotions, uniqueness, personality and understanding of your purpose in life.

To score the Self-Understanding Scale total your score for each section and put that score on the line marked Total. Then transfer them to each of the scales below.

I. **What Triggers My Emotions**   **Total** = _____

II. **What Makes Me Unique**   **Total** = _____

III. **What Is My Personality**   **Total** = _____

IV. **What is My Life Purpose**   **Total** = _____

Profile Interpretation

Individual Scale Score	Result	Indications
10 to 16	low	Your score indicates that you are not very self-aware. It will be helpful for you to learn more about yourself.
17 to 23	moderate	Your score indicates that you are somewhat self-aware. It will be helpful for you to better understand yourself.
24 to 30	high	Your score indicates that you are very self-aware. Continue to retain and improve your self-understanding.

The higher you score on the Self-Understanding Scale, the more self-aware you are and the more you truly understand yourself. No matter if you scored in the **Low**, **Moderate** or **High** range, the exercises and activities that follow are designed to help you learn to increase your self-understanding even more.

Teen Self-Understanding Scale Descriptions

What Triggers My Emotions

People scoring high on this scale are able to quickly and easily recognize their emotions. They understand how their emotions can affect their life both in positive and negative ways. They see the connection of their emotions, thinking and behavior. They understand he events and situations that trigger their emotions, and they can easily control those emotional triggers.

What Makes Me Unique

People scoring high on this scale are able to quickly and easily understand their uniqueness as human beings. They understand their strengths and weaknesses, skills and abilities, and unique talents. They view themselves as special in many different ways, and they are able to use their uniqueness to make a difference in the world. They also are interested in learning all they can to overcome their weaknesses.

What Is My Personality

People scoring high on this scale understand their unique personality traits. They understand what makes them a one-of-a-kind person. They understand their personality traits, their unique outlook, their temperament, and the situations that can make them happy or sad. They understand how their personality traits can bring people closer to them and also push others away.

What Is My Life Purpose

People scoring high on this scale understand that they have a unique purpose in life, and are committed to fulfill this purpose. They are aware of what they value most and try to bring those values to everything they do. They are interested in identifying and expressing their purpose in their lives.

Emotional Understanding

The first step to better understand your emotions is to explore the emotions you experienced during the week and to explore what was happening in your life at the time. Remember that your feelings are not caused by situations in which you find yourself or people with whom you interact. *You choose how to react to your feelings*.

The following exercise will help you to begin to understand the emotions you have recently experienced and what was occurring in your life when you had these feelings. Think back upon the past week. Reflect on the emotions you experienced each day and what you were doing when you experienced them.

Days	Feelings experienced and what were you doing when you experienced them
Monday	
Tuesday	
Wednesday	
Thursday	
Friday	
Saturday	
Sunday	

Emotional Understanding Review

After reviewing your last week, what emotions, negative or positive, did you experience the most and with whom?

Emotion	With whom (name code)

What conclusions can you come to after looking at the above table?

_____

_____

Ways I am Unique

You are a unique human being. It is important to understand the various ways that you are unique. Select and identify the areas where you feel you have a unique talent, skill or ability and write the ways you are special and unique.

	Ways I am unique
Physically	
Intellectually	
Spiritually	
Emotionally	
Creatively	
Personally	
Other	

Well and Not-So-Well

To better understand your unique purpose in life, you need to take a look at the things you do well and the things you don't do very well. The most talented people have things they don't do very well. By focusing on your strengths, or working hard on things you love to do, but don't do very well, you will have a greater chance of living your life in accordance with your unique purpose.

I do this well ...

Ex: I am able to express my thoughts and feelings best with poetry.

_____

_____

_____

_____

_____

_____

_____

_____

_____

I don't do this very well ...

Ex: I am awful in math – and I don't like it. I take the classes I must take and I try.

_____

_____

_____

_____

_____

_____

_____

_____

_____

Insights about Me!

Without giving these sentence starters much thought, just read the words and answer with your first response.

I never expected

_____

_____

_____

_____

An unusual day in my life

_____

_____

_____

_____

The best gift I ever received

_____

_____

_____

_____

The worst gift I ever received

_____

_____

_____

_____

(Continued on the next page)

Insights about Me! *(page 2)*

I wish I weren't so _____

_____

_____

_____

_____

One of my most important goals _____

_____

_____

_____

_____

I really miss _____

_____

_____

_____

_____

What makes me feel proud _____

_____

_____

_____

_____

(Continued on the next page)

Insights about Me! *(page 3)*

I'm glad I'm alive when

_____

_____

_____

_____

_____

I am grateful

_____

_____

_____

_____

I sometimes forget to be grateful for

_____

_____

_____

_____

When I need time for myself

_____

_____

_____

_____

(Continued on the next page)

Insights about Me! *(page 4)*

I wish

_____

_____

_____

_____

_____

I dream that one day

_____

_____

_____

_____

_____

I am

_____

_____

_____

_____

_____

By next year, I hope

_____

_____

_____

_____

(Continued on the next page)

Insights about Me! *(page 5)*

Few people realize I

_____

_____

_____

_____

I hope

_____

_____

_____

_____

I do not

_____

_____

_____

_____

Each day

_____

_____

_____

_____

(Continued on the next page)

Insights about Me! *(page 6)*

It hurts when

_____

_____

_____

_____

_____

When I need to choose

_____

_____

_____

_____

_____

I never

_____

_____

_____

_____

_____

I love

_____

_____

_____

_____

_____

Quotations ~ Self-Understanding

The following quotations pertain to self-understanding. Choose one and check it off. Write about how it relates to you.

❏ *Hide not your talents, they for use were made. What's a sundial in the shade?*

~ Benjamin Franklin

❏ *No one can make you feel inferior without your consent.*

~ Eleanor Roosevelt

❏ *I was brought up to believe that how I saw myself was more important than how others saw me.*

~ Anwar el-Sadat

❏ *Be a first rate version of yourself, not a second rate version of someone else.*

~ Judy Garland

_____

_____

_____

_____

_____

_____

_____

_____

_____

_____

_____

_____

_____

_____

Understanding Myself

After completing this chapter, how do you know yourself better?

_____
_____
_____
_____
_____
_____
_____
_____
_____
_____
_____
_____

How can you learn even more about yourself?

_____
_____
_____
_____
_____
_____
_____
_____
_____
_____
_____
_____

Facts about Self-Understanding

- Self-understanding comes from being aware of my thoughts, feelings, and behaviors.

- Self-awareness and self-understanding are necessary for growth and change.

- Self-understanding includes recognizing why I behave in both positive and negative ways.

- Self-understanding is being able to focus and pay attention to myself and to my relationship with the world around me.

- Self-understanding comes from becoming more aware of myself, even if I don't like what I find out.

~ You are now on the path of self-understanding. You may not like everything you have discovered about yourself, but self-understanding allows for the opportunity to grow and change. ~

When I Understand Myself

I am aware of ...

- my unique qualities

- my talents

- my skills

- my personality

- my purpose in life

- my emotional reactions to certain situations

- my emotional reactions to certain people

- my strengths

- my weaknesses

SECTION V:

Teen Self-Responsibility Scale

Name_____

Date_____

Teen Self-Responsibility Scale
Directions

Self-responsibility is acknowledging that you, and you alone, are responsible for your thoughts, feelings and behaviors. It is the awareness that YOU are the person responsible for what happens in your life. Self-responsibility is refusing to view yourself as a victim powerless over what happens to you. It means not blaming others or your past.

The *Teen Self-Responsibility Scale* can help you determine how much control you have in life, how trustworthy you are and how much integrity you demonstrate. This assessment contains 28 statements. Read each of the statements and decide how much you agree with the statement. Circle the number of your response on the line to the right of each statement. Pay no attention to the numbers, only to the headings on top.

In the following example, the circled 1 indicates that the person completing the scale strongly agreed with the statement:

	Strongly Agree	Agree	Disagree	Strongly Disagree
1. I usually finish what I start	(1)	2	3	4

This is not a test and there are no right or wrong answers. Do not spend too much time thinking about your answers. Your initial response will be the most true for you. Be sure to respond to every statement.

(Turn to the next page and begin)

Teen Self-Responsibility Scale

	Strongly Agree	Agree	Disagree	Strongly Disagree
1. I usually finish what I start	4	3	2	1
2. I always try to do what is right.	4	3	2	1
3. I keep my promises.	4	3	2	1
4. I often speak unkindly of others	1	2	3	4
5. I am sometimes unreliable	1	2	3	4
6. I am true to myself	4	3	2	1
7. I am strongly committed to the people in my life	4	3	2	1
8. I am calm under pressure	4	3	2	1
9. My friends can depend on me.	4	3	2	1
10. I have my values.	4	3	2	1
11. Others know I am a person of my word	4	3	2	1
12. I control my temper	4	3	2	1
13. I fulfill my obligations.	4	3	2	1
14. I often give in to temptations	1	2	3	4
15. I follow through on my commitments	4	3	2	1
16. I get angry at others	1	2	3	4
17. I tend to blame others for my problems	1	2	3	4
18. When I say I'll be somewhere, I am always on time . . .	4	3	2	1
19. I am an honest person	4	3	2	1
20. I tend to sulk when I don't get my way.	1	2	3	4
21. I am accountable for my actions.	4	3	2	1
22. I am able to overcome obstacles in my life.	4	3	2	1
23. I have betrayed secrets in the past	1	2	3	4
24. I can control my emotions	4	3	2	1
25. I rarely think about the consequences of my actions . .	1	2	3	4
26. I rarely compromise my values.	4	3	2	1
27. I am loyal to other people.	4	3	2	1
28. I let other people upset me.	1	2	3	4

(Go to the Scoring Directions on the next page)

Teen Self-Responsibility Scale
Scoring Directions

The *Teen Self-Responsibility Scale* is designed to measure your level of self-responsibility. Four areas have been identified which describe various aspects of self-responsibility: Responsibility, Integrity, Trustworthiness and Control. Items which comprise each of the four scales are grouped so that you may explore how responsible you are.

To score the assessment look at the items on the previous page. Use the spaces below to transfer and record the number which you circled on each individual item.

Responsibility		Integrity		Trustworthy		Control	
Item #	Score	Item #	Score	Item #	Score	Item #	Score
1	_____	2	_____	3	_____	4	_____
5	_____	6	_____	7	_____	8	_____
9	_____	10	_____	11	_____	12	_____
13	_____	14	_____	15	_____	16	_____
17	_____	18	_____	19	_____	20	_____
21	_____	22	_____	23	_____	24	_____
25	_____	26	_____	27	_____	28	_____
Total = _____		Total = _____		Total = _____		Total = _____	

(Go to the Profile Interpretation on the next page)

Teen Self-Responsibility Scale Profile Interpretation

Individual Scale Score	Result	Indications
7 to 13	low	You often do not take responsibility for yourself and your life. You show a low level of integrity and do not demonstrate control. You show that others cannot trust you.
14 to 21	moderate	You tend to take some responsibility for yourself and your life. You try to show integrity and demonstrate some control. You usually can be trusted by others.
22 to 28	high	You tend to take full responsibility for yourself and your life, show integrity, demonstrate control, and you can be trusted by others.

For any scales in which you scored in the "Low" or "Moderate" ranges, find that description on the pages that follow. Then, you should read the description and complete the exercises that are included. These exercises will help you to enhance your self-responsibility in life.

Scale Descriptions

SCALE I – Responsibility: People scoring high on this scale tend to take responsibility for what happens in their lives. They feel they have the freedom and responsibility to make the choices that determine the outcomes in their life choices.

SCALE II – Integrity: People scoring high on this scale show integrity in their daily lives. They do what is right, model ethical behavior, and remain true to their values. They do their best and are rarely tempted to stray from their values.

SCALE III – Trustworthy: People scoring high on this scale can trust themselves and be trusted by other people. They keep their promises and are committed to positive action. They keep their word and follow through when they give their word.

SCALE IV – Control: People scoring high on this scale take control for what happens in their lives. They are calm under pressure, control their emotions, and remain calm when other people try to upset them.

Responsibility and Me

Accepting responsibility means that you are able to take greater control of your life. Responsibility includes being able to take advantage of life's opportunities and cope with life's challenges. Teens who are responsible make valuable, productive decisions that keep them on course. They take appropriate action until they get the results they want. This helps them achieve leadership roles. When teens show responsibility, people know they are reliable.

Accepting responsibility means that you are responsible for all aspects of your life. You accept the bad as well as the good. You are responsible for what you do now, who you are and what you will do in the future. Sometimes people find themselves in a bad situation. Our reactions to these circumstances and events, and the decisions that we make, are important. In the table that follows, identify the ways you will begin being more responsible in the various aspects of your life. Use name codes.

Areas of My Life	How I Will Be More Responsible
My Behaviors	
My Thoughts	
My Actions	
My Reactions	
My Education	

(Continued on the nest page)

Responsibility and Me *(Continued)*

Areas of My Life	How I Will Be More Responsible
My Family	
My Friends	
What I Say and How I Say It	
Finishing What I Start	
Fulfilling My Obligations	
Keeping my Word	
Integrity	
Honesty	
Sticking to My Own Values	

My Responsibility Story

In what ways are you responsible?

_____

_____

_____

In what ways are you irresponsible?

_____

_____

_____

How does being responsible affect your relationships with friends?

_____

_____

_____

How does being responsible affect your relationships with your family?

_____

_____

_____

Think about someone you know, one whom you can count on no matter what. How does that person demonstrate that responsibility?

_____

_____

_____

Write about a time you showed responsibility.

_____

_____

_____

Integrity and Me

How do you maintain your standards and values?

_____

_____

_____

Describe some situations where you did the right thing even though it was difficult for you. In the left-hand column describe the situation and in the right-hand column describe what you did.

Situation	How I Acted with Integrity
Ex: Someone was being bullied. Everyone stood around and watched.	_I left and got an adult who intervened without disclosing that it was me who told._

My Integrity Story

What choices have you made that are consistent with your values?

_____

_____

_____

_____

What choices have you made that are not consistent with your values?

_____

_____

_____

_____

For what do you want to be remembered?

_____

_____

_____

_____

What are you doing to be remembered in this way?

_____

_____

_____

_____

What are you doing to keep you from being remembered in the way you hope?

_____

_____

_____

_____

Trustworthiness and Me

Think about the promises that you have kept in the past and those that you have not kept. In the tables that follow, describe those situations. Use name codes.

Promises I Have Kept
Ex: I told TM I would clean up while she was working, and I did a great job.

Promises I Have Not Kept
Ex: I told NZ that I would help her with homework last night and I chose to go out with a friend instead. I didn't even call!

My Trustworthy Story

How do your friends and family know whether you can be trusted?

_____

_____

_____

_____

What are the situations in which you find yourself less than honest?

_____

_____

_____

_____

To whom are you loyal?

_____

_____

_____

_____

What promises or commitments have you not followed through on?

_____

_____

_____

_____

Who is someone whose trust you want, but know the trust has been broken? How can you regain that trust?

_____

_____

_____

_____

Control of My Emotions and Me

Think about areas of your life where you lose control of your emotions, lose your patience, and/or act out in a way that embarrassed you. Below, describe how you lose control.

Areas of My Life	How I Lose Control
Ex: Competitions	*Ex: I hate to lose, and when I do, I storm around and I am mean*
Competitions	
School	
Work / Volunteer	
Dating	
Family	
Friends	
Community	
Driving	
Sports	
Aggressive people	
Other	

My Emotions and Control Story

In what ways could you better control your emotions?

_____

_____

_____

_____

In what situations do you lack self-control?

_____

_____

_____

_____

In what situations do you lose your temper?

_____

_____

_____

_____

In what situations do you stay calm?

_____

_____

_____

_____

In what situations are you unable to maintain self-control, stay calm and/or not lose your temper?

_____

_____

_____

_____

Putting it All Together

Review ways you have not behaved responsibly. Then explore ways you will be more responsible. Use name codes.

Aspects of Self-Responsibility	My Behavior in the Past	How I will Behave in the Future
Ex: Responsibility	I would say I'd do something and then not show up, call or apologize.	I'm not going to make a commitment unless I know I can do it. If anything happens I'll call or text and be sure they receive it.
Responsibility		
Integrity		
Trustworthiness		
Control of Emotions		

Self-Responsibility Quotations

The following quotations relate to self-responsibility. Choose one and check it off. Write about how it relates to something that has happened in your life or in the life of someone else you know.

❏ *The willingness to accept responsibility for one's own life is the source from which self-respect springs.*

~ **Joan Didion**

❏ *Action springs not from thought, but from a readiness for responsibility.*

~ **Dietrich Bonhoeffer**

❏ *Take your life in your own hands, and what happens? A terrible thing: no one to blame.*

~ **Erica Jong**

❏ *We are made wise not by the recollection of our past, but by the responsibility for our future.*

~ **George Bernard Shaw**

_____

_____

_____

_____

_____

_____

_____

_____

_____

_____

_____

_____

_____

_____

_____

_____

Taking Responsibility

How have you blamed others so that you can avoid taking responsibility for your actions?
Use name codes.

_____

_____

_____

_____

_____

_____

_____

How have you made excuses to avoid taking responsibility for your actions?
Use name codes.

_____

_____

_____

_____

_____

_____

_____

Write about being ready to stop blaming others or making excuses, and instead, being ready
to become a responsible citizen.

_____

_____

_____

_____

_____

_____

_____

Commitments

How have you followed-through on your commitments?

_____

_____

_____

_____

_____

_____

_____

_____

_____

How haven't you followed-through on your commitments?

_____

_____

_____

_____

_____

_____

_____

_____

_____

Write about being ready to start honoring every commitment that you make.

_____

_____

_____

_____

_____

_____

_____

_____

_____

Responsibility

It's time for me to take responsibility for . . .

- My choice of friends

- My educational goals

- My healthy choices

- My integrity, honesty and dependability

- My own life

- My being true to my values

- My motivation

- My physical, mental and emotional health

- My setting goals and reaching them

- My successes and failures

- My willingness to care for and help others

Self-Responsibility is...

- Accepting reality

- Accepting myself fully

- Loving myself unconditionally

- Appreciating my personal worth

- Setting attainable goals for myself

- Keeping my emotions under control

- Believing completely that
  I am important

- Knowing that I am unique

- Taking responsibility for what happens
  to me

- Feeling comfortable within my mind,
  body and soul

- Acknowledging and respecting my
  rights and the rights of others